British Open Champions

About the Author

Michael Hobbs is a freelance writer who has written or edited over twenty books on golf, half-a-dozen of them with Peter Alliss. He has contributed to *The Times*, the *Guardian* and many of the world's leading golf publications including *Golf World* for whom he writes on golf history and memorabilia. He has published several books on the history of the game as a partner in Grant Books and operates a golf picture library from his home in Northumberland.

British Open Champions

MICHAEL HOBBS

CHAPMANS
1991

CHAPMANS LIBRARY OF GOLF

Editor Tim Jollands
Designer Humphrey Stone

Chapmans Publishers Ltd
141-143 Drury Lane
London WC2B 5TB

A CIP Catalogue record
for this book is available from
the British Library

ISBN 1 85592 556 7

First published by Chapmans in 1991
Copyright © Michael Hobbs and
Jollands Editions 1991

Text set in Palatino
Typeset by Character Graphics,
Taunton, Somerset
Printed in Spain for Imago

CONTENTS

PREFACE

One of my ambitions has been to write a book that dealt in part or wholly with the early years of the Open Championship. These were times when there must have been immense pleasure in winning but from the perspective of 1991 it really was a parish affair. Those who had the fare, or a caddying engagement with the gentry, would only consider entering if the event was being held just a few miles away. You played if it was at Musselburgh, and you lived there, but few would venture the relatively short journey from the east of Scotland to Prestwick in the west. A century or more later, as we all know, it is very different.

The thanks I would like to express are to do with my writing about those early years of the championship. Everyone knows the names of the Parks and the Morrises as well as the Watsons and Nicklauses. But what of Jack Simpson, Tom Kidd and Jack Burns? I think it is true to say that no one has much expertise about these far-off achievements but in this context I am particularly indebted to Peter Crabtree for his considerable efforts in searching through his extensive golf library and to John Adams, the author of a book on the Park family. I would also like to thank Bobby Burnet, historian to the R&A, who has been particularly willing to delve into the R&A Library to establish in several instances the birth and death dates of our Open Champions.

MICHAEL HOBBS
Stocksfield
July 1991

INTRODUCTION

The first golf championship of any kind took place at St Andrews in 1857. The format was foursomes with clubs being invited to enter one pair each. It was won by two Scots from the Blackheath club in England. The next two years, the event was played by matchplay singles and then the National Amateur Tournament faded away.

A little earlier, in 1856, the Prestwick club on the west coast of Scotland had suggested an event for professionals but apparently met with no response from other clubs. Prestwick decided to go it alone. Perhaps they had a particularly strong interest because they had the likely winner in their professional, Tom Morris.

The first event took place on 17 October 1860. It counts as the first Open Championship although it was hardly 'open'. The contest was not at all widely publicised and it hadn't been considered that amateurs might wish to take part. Instead, the terms laid down that any professional could enter, provided they were 'known and respectable cadies' [sic]. This was changed for 1861 when it was 'unanimously resolved that the challenge belt tomorrow until it be otherwise resolved shall be open to all the world'.

So it has continued to be. The trophy of a red Morocco belt set with silver ornamentation did not, however, survive for long. The rules laid down that anyone winning three in a row should retain the belt. In 1868-70, Young Tom Morris did just that. After a gap of a year, the championship resumed with a new trophy, the claret jug which survives to this day, with Morris's the first name inscribed on it. He remains the only man to win the title four consecutive years, one of a handful with a claim to be considered amongst the very greatest golfers.

The number of competitors that first year of 1860 was just eight. This changed little for quite some time. The Open was just a part of Prestwick's Autumn Meeting and, with the mass of golf being played on the eastern side of Scotland, the venue was remote enough to deter men with little or no money to spare. After 1872, however, the championship was also played at Musselburgh and St Andrews and fields, if not consistently, gradually grew in size.

Scottish dominance of the event was not long-lived. In 1890 the first Englishman, the amateur John Ball, won and another English amateur,

Harold Hilton, took two titles in the 1890s. As early as 1893, in fact, Willie Auchterlonie became the last Scottish born, bred nd resident champion. Then came the dominance of the 'Great Triumvirate' of Harry Vardon, James Braid and J.H. Taylor, who took 16 titles between 1894 and 1914, with Vardon's six still the record.

After the First World War their day was done and the 1920s, through Walter Hagen and Bobby Jones, was a period of American ascendancy. Eventually, especially as the US Tour developed, fewer competitors came from across the Atlantic. Henry Cotton of England was always the most likely winner in the 1930s and for a few years after the Second World War. Then the Commonwealth took over from 1949 to 1959 with South African Bobby Locke taking the championship four times and Peter Thomson of Australia also winning four, including three in a row, a feat not accomplished since Bob Ferguson in 1882. The first of South African Gary Player's three victories came in 1959 and Thomson added a fifth title in 1965.

By this time American interest was beginning to revive though for a while US Tour players saw the Open as something which interested Arnold Palmer and Jack Nicklaus. The rest went off to play a Tour event as usual. This attitude gradually changed. By the early 1970s most of the best Americans were competing and today the Open can be said to be a part of the US Tour as regards scheduling.

For quite some time as the Open developed there was more press and public interest in the Amateur Championship, which began in 1885. Even if the fields were not quite so strong, club golfers were more concerned about the doings of their fellow amateurs and liked the cut and thrust of matchplay golf. There was also the point that virtually no amateur gave the slightest thought to turning professional. Except for the very greatest players, professionals were seen primarily as servants of golf club memberships. A leading amateur was likely to make a great deal more money out of the game and had far more prestige. Today, alas, the Amateur can no longer be considered a major championship; the most promising players are usually quick to join the professional ranks.

Of the other championships considered 'majors' today, the US Open ranks next in order of seniority, having been first played in 1895. For some years it was dominated by British-born players who had emigrated to the United States and native superiority was not established until much the same time as Americans began to dominate the Open Championship. Next came the USPGA Championship, first played in 1916 and a fascinating event until in 1958 it moved from matchplay to strokeplay to suit the demands of television. Today it is undoubtedly a very important event but I doubt that you would find a professional who would rather win it in preference to the Open, the US Open or the Masters.

[8]

The Masters is an oddity, the only one of the four majors that is a championship of nothing at all. It grew in importance quickly because of the enormous prestige of Bobby Jones, who helped found the tournament and the course where it is played, Augusta National. The fact that it is always at the same venue has been helpful - the last nine holes at Augusta must be the best known piece of golfing terrain in the world.

Terrain also helps to make the Open so distinctive. Every course that has hosted the championship is laid out over linksland and this will surely never change even if the finest course in the world were to be created on, say, Scottish moorland or the heaths of Surrey.

There is no need for us to decide which is the greatest among the three majors (having unkindly dismissed the USPGA). Most American players would prefer a US Open or a Masters title on their record while Europeans would choose the Open. In part, this is because far more money falls into the lap of a top player who wins in his own backyard.

For my money, however, the Open is the greatest event in the golfing year because it has by far the most international field. The championship, since 1861, has been 'open to all the world' and the R&A is very concerned to make sure that the leading players of all the world tours and circuits have direct entry without having to pre-qualify. By comparison, the US Open and the Masters seem preoccupied with keeping 'foreigners' out rather than encouraging world-class fields.

WILLIE PARK SNR

1860 1863 1866 1875

Born Musselburgh, Midlothian (1834 to 1903). The first great player to come from the caddie ranks, rather than a background in club and ball making (which he took to later), Park first appeared on the golfing scene in 1854. In this year, for stakes of £100, he challenged Allan Robertson (the greatest player of his time), Tom Morris or Willie Dunn. George Morris played instead and was beaten by many holes, causing Robertson to say: 'Willie frichtens us wi' his long driving.' Brother Tom then took up the challenge over 36 holes and lost by five holes. This was the first of many matches between Park and Morris when such events were far more keenly followed than the Open Championship. When this began in 1860, after Robertson's death, Park got home by a couple of strokes from Morris and the pair dominated the event until the arrival of Young Tom Morris. Besides his victories, Park was also second four times.

Park learned to play the game with one club, a curved stick, and with it became a long and straight driver and excellent putter. How it would have served him in bunkers we cannot know as it is said that he always managed to avoid them. Such was his flair for the game that he would often play club golfers using only one hand and standing on one leg. He lost only once. On another occasion, he accepted a challenge to play a round playing all his tee shots from a watch face. The watch was unscathed at the end.

OLD TOM MORRIS

1861 1862 1864 1867

Born St Andrews, Fife (1821 to 1908). Tom Morris wanted to be a carpenter but was persuaded that the craft of making feathery balls and golf clubs had better prospects. He was apprenticed at 18 to Allan Robertson and later stayed on with him as a journeyman. They formed an unbeaten partnership in the challenge matches of the time and their recovery against the Dunns of Musselburgh in 1849, over four greens for stakes of £400, has passed into golfing legend. A few months later they parted company when Robertson saw Morris using the new gutta-percha ball – Robertson, fearing the loss of his feathery trade, had burned any gutty he could find and spoke of the new ball with contempt. Morris set up on his own and in 1851 accepted the job of Prestwick's first Keeper of the Green.

Morris was a steady rather than inspirational player and he managed to prosper without being long off the tee or a good short putter (an envelope addressed to 'The Misser of Short Putts, Prestwick' failed to trouble the postman). He won four of the first eight Opens and continued to play in the Open until he was 75; at 46 years 99 days he remains the oldest champion. Returning to St Andrews as Keeper of the Green (1864 to 1904), Old Tom set up a successful clubmaking firm and can also be considered the first golf architect: many of our great courses (later much changed) were laid out by him, including the scene of his Open triumphs, Prestwick, and Muirfield.

ANDREW STRATH

1865

Top professionals at a tournament at Leith Links in 1867: (left to right) Andrew Strath,
Davie Park, Bob Kirk, Jamie Anderson, Jamie Dunn, Willie Dow, Willie Dunn,
Alexander Greig, Old Tom, Young Tom and George Morris

Born St Andrews, Fife (1836 to 1868). Though not perhaps quite as good a player as his brother Davie, it was Andrew who became an Open champion. His victory broke the alternation between Old Tom Morris and Willie Park Snr as champions. He won in style: his 162 for three rounds over Prestwick's 12 holes was the lowest in the championship until the advent of Young Tom Morris. His winning card is the earliest to survive.

Strath was a St Andrews man and started golf as an apprentice with James Wilson, successor to the great clubmaker Hugh Philp. As a golfer he was famous for the amount of backspin he could get on his iron shots. Old Tom Morris would sometimes choose him as a foursomes partner in the money matches which were such a feature of golf at this time.

In his short career, Strath had a very good record in the Open. He was third in 1860, fourth in 1863, second in 1864 and fourth in 1867. In 1865 he succeeded Old Tom Morris as Keeper of the Green at Prestwick but died of tuberculosis at the age of 32. His brother Davie also died young, while a third brother, George, emigrated to the United States after serving as Troon's first professional. The Strath bunker guarding the 11th green on the Old Course offers a permanent reminder of one of St Andrews' most famous families. It might have got its name because contemporaries thought Andrew often found sand, perhaps this bunker in particular.

YOUNG TOM MORRIS

1868 1869 1870 1872

Born St Andrews, Fife (1851 to 1875). 'Tommy' Morris eclipsed his contemporaries and totally changed their conception of how well the game could be played – like Vardon, Jones and Hogan in later generations. He excelled in all parts of the game. A powerful striker who was occasionally wild with his driving, he could rip his recoveries from the resulting bad lies. His iron play was revolutionary: he used the small-headed rut iron as a pitching club, obtaining increased backspin by playing off the back foot. His putting – on the poor greens of the time – amazed others for its boldness from a distance and its consistency from close up.

He won his first Open at 17, succeeding his father as champion. He remains the youngest winner and is the only golfer to have won four in a row. (There was no championship in 1871 as Morris had won the trophy, a fine Morocco belt, outright due to his hat-trick of victories. The present silver claret jug was not available until 1872.) His victory margins were 5, 11, 12 and 3 strokes and his average per round, the equivalent of 74½, was unbeaten even by the Triumvirate during the era of the gutty. His first-round 47 in 1870 was one of the greatest rounds of golf ever played.

At the age of 24, Young Tom died from a lung haemorrhage on Christmas Day, 1875, just three months after his wife had died while giving birth to their still-born child.

[13]

TOM KIDD

1873

Born St Andrews, Fife (1848 to 1884). After Young Tom Morris won his third title in 1870, the Open took a year off as there was no trophy to play for. When the championship resumed for the present claret jug it was no longer an entirely Prestwick affair, for the R&A and the Honourable Company of Edinburgh Golfers had contributed to the costs of the new trophy and future championships were to be played at St Andrews and Musselburgh as well as Prestwick.

The first St Andrews event was held in 1873 and was won by Tom Kidd who, like his father, was an Old Course caddie. With scores of 91 and 88 and an aggregate of 179, the somewhat ungainly but long-hitting Kidd's total was the highest recorded while the championship was played over 36 holes. His 88 was, even so, the lowest round all day. The weather was fine but the course was covered in pools of water after heavy rain during the days leading up to the championship – hence the high scoring.

Tom Kidd, as well as being the first St Andrews champion, also became the first man to halt the dominance of Morris, who finished four strokes behind, tied for third place, with Kidd beating future champion Jamie Anderson by one stroke. Kidd was eighth at Musselburgh the following year, fifth in 1879 at St Andrews and 11th in 1882 on the same course. It is highly likely that he didn't enter the Prestwick events because of the travel involved.

MUNGO PARK

1874

Born Musselburgh, Midlothian (1835 to 1904). Less well known than his brother Willie Park Snr, Mungo might well have achieved greater golfing fame if he had not spent many of his peak years at sea. On his return he was quick to win the Open, held in 1874 for the first time at Musselburgh. A fine putter in the Park tradition, Mungo partnered his brother in many money matches. It was after their match against Old and Young Tom Morris at North Berwick in 1875 that Young Tom received the message that his wife was dangerously ill. She died before his return to St Andrews.

In 1877 or 1878, Mungo went as professional to what is now Alnmouth Village GC. In 1879 he made the first course for Tyneside GC before returning to Alnmouth, for which he had great affection. He said he wanted to be buried under a seat where golfers looked out to sea so that he could listen to them talking golf. It is said that he once played a local clergyman at Alnmouth where his side-stake was to take the pledge for six months if he lost. He managed to hole a long putt for a half on the last. Offered a re-match he replied: 'No thanks. It's been ower close this time.'

A good ball and club maker, Mungo Park eventually left Alnmouth in 1890 and went to work in north-west England, being greenkeeper at Silloth for a while. His career emphasises that being Open champion was no passport to fame and fortune.

BOB MARTIN

1876 1885

Born South Toll, Fife (1848 to c1914). Bob Martin is the only man to have been given a 'walkover' in the Open. In 1876, Davie Strath needed to finish his last round at St Andrews with two 5s to win. He got his 5 at the dreaded Road hole but took 6 on the last. There would have to be a play-off the next day. Or would there? Playing his third on the 17th, Strath struck a player on the green. (The game ahead of Strath consisted of ordinary players out for a round, some illustration of the status of the Open at the time.) There were calls for his disqualification. The committee announced that the play-off would go ahead the next day without the protest having been decided. Strath refused to play. Bob Martin appeared on time, walked the course and was declared champion.

In 1885, again at St Andrews, Martin finished a stroke ahead of Archie Simpson and two ahead of David Ayton, whose alleged 11 at the Road hole in the first round has been proved incorrect. Martin's two wins should not, therefore, be regarded as flukes; he also had several other high finishes in the Open including second places in 1875 and 1887.

Martin began caddying about the age of 11 and then went into clubmaking. As a golfer he first made a name for himself by emerging from working as a shepherd to win a tournament with Young Tom Morris in the field. Martin reckoned he had three times played the Old Course in 75.

JAMIE ANDERSON

1877 1878 1879

Born St Andrews, Fife (1842 to 1905). Only Young Tom Morris has ever managed to win four consecutive Opens. Others have come close, notably Peter Thomson and Bob Ferguson, but Jamie Anderson missed out for a very odd reason. Notice of the championship date was given so late that he did not even play in 1880. The following year he was second and in 1882 he tied for third place, an impressive run of high placings.

Anderson put in one of golf's most dramatic finishes to win at Prestwick in 1878. J.O.F. Morris, a son of Old Tom, was in with a total of 161. Jamie had to play the last four holes in 17 strokes and thought 5, 4, 3, 5 would do it. He did not play the 15th too well but holed a long iron shot for a 3. On the 17th his tee shot hit a bank by the green and trickled into the hole. Having beaten Morris by four strokes, further luck was needed when Bob Kirk put in a storming finish, had a putt to tie on the last and nearly holed it.

Anderson, the son of 'Old Daw' whose ginger-beer stall gave the name to the 4th hole at St Andrews, was a deadly player of the approach shot and very consistent. He once claimed that he had played 90 holes without a bad shot. In money matches, he just waited for opponents to make mistakes. There was no real money in the game until the advent of the Great Triumvirate and, like so many professionals of the time, his end was not a happy one. He died in a poor house in Perth.

BOB FERGUSON

1880 1881 1882

Born Musselburgh, Midlothian (1848 to 1915). This triple Open champion first made a name for himself at the age of 18 when, with a few borrowed clubs, he beat the cream of the professionals in the Leith Tournament. His 131 for four rounds of Leith's seven holes so impressed a local admirer that he paid for new clubs which Ferguson used for the rest of his career. He took part in several challenge matches against Young Tom Morris and usually came off second best although he did once win by four holes when the pair used cleeks only.

After a few good performances in the Open, including third place in 1869, Ferguson's first victory came at his native Musselburgh, by five strokes. His next wins, at Prestwick (in appalling weather) and St Andrews, were, with their three-stroke margins, also decisive. Could he equal Young Tom Morris by taking four in a row? He came very close. He tied Willie Fernie, finishing with three 3s, and in the 36 hole play-off was one stroke to the good standing on the last tee. Though a par 4, it was drivable that day. Ferguson got his par but Fernie sank a long putt for a 2.

A little later he contracted typhoid and played no more competitive golf. He became Custodian of the Links at Musselburgh and taught the boys of Loretto School golf. If they failed to follow his instructions he was apt to rap them across the calves with a club shaft.

[18]

WILLIE FERNIE

1883

Born St Andrews, Fife (1857 to 1924). For some twenty years from the late 1870s until the turn of the century, Fernie seemed almost always able to raise his game for the Open. Amongst his numerous high placings he finished in second place four times (1882, 1884, 1890 and 1891) and tied third behind Vardon and Taylor in 1896.

A plasterer by trade, Fernie rose to prominence as a golfer in the competitions of the St Andrews Artisan Club. From about 1880 he began to win now-long-forgotten tournaments. During one of these at Alnmouth, one of the earliest English golf clubs, he and Willie Park Jnr were tied after 36 holes. Out they went the next day for another 36. Again they tied and – no sudden death for TV cameras then – they had to play another 36. It was almost as close this time too but Fernie came through to win by a stroke.

Fernie's single Open Championship victory prevented Bob Ferguson winning four in a row. The pair tied, despite Fernie taking 10 on one hole. In the play-off, he holed a long 'steal' (putt) for a 2 on the last while Ferguson, with a stroke lead, managed only a par 4.

After spells at Dumfries, Felixstowe and Ardeer, Fernie served as Troon's professional from 1887 until the year of his death. In addition to alterations at Troon, he was responsible for laying out several courses, notably the original Ailsa and Arran courses at Turnberry.

JACK SIMPSON

1884

Born Earlsferry, Fife (c1858 to 1895). The eldest of six golfing brothers, Jack was probably not quite as good a player as his brother Archie but he won the Open Championship. A stonemason from Elie, he emerged as the best player in the Elie Thistle club. A superb long driver, he was as inconsistent as he was brilliant. In one tournament over Carnoustie he drove into the rough, topped his next two shots horribly and then hit an enormous shot followed by a superb pitch stone dead. After that, he missed the putt for a half. The most powerful player of his day, it is said that he sometimes buckled the heads of irons after just a few shots.

Simpson's play on the 2nd hole at Prestwick in his winning year would have had many competitors tearing up their cards. He topped his drive into some whins virtually under his nose and stumbled to a 9. But he was renowned for, and accustomed to, his bad starts. He continued serenely to a 78 to take the lead and won the championship by four strokes.

Jack had no other high finishes in the Open. The following year he trailed behind his brothers Archie (second) and Bob (equal fourth). Whereas Archie would compete in the Open for another twenty years, Jack died young and it seems that he concentrated mainly on clubmaking in Elie, having learned the skills from Archie. The family name survives on the golf shop just across the road from the Carnoustie courses.

DAVID BROWN

1886

Born Musselburgh, Midlothian (1860 to c1929). The tournament professional of today arrives at events with an extensive wardrobe. Not so David Brown for the 1886 Open at Musselburgh. Not having intended even to enter, he came straight from his work as a slater. He was filthy and in his work clothes. It wouldn't do. So they gave him a bath in the clubhouse and fitted him out in striped trousers, a frock coat and a lum hat. He totalled 157 for four rounds of the nine-hole course to beat Willie Campbell by two strokes. His aggregate was the lowest for Musselburgh Opens at the time and had only been bettered elsewhere by Young Tom Morris.

Up to the time of his victory, it looks as if 'Deacon' Brown entered the championship only when it was being played at Musselburgh. He had tied fourth in 1880 and achieved the same placing over his home course in 1889. He produced several strong performances in later Opens while professional to the Worcestershire GC, one of the earliest in England.

His greatest achievement in later years came in the 1903 US Open at Baltusrol after he had emigrated around the turn of the century, like so many other Scottish professionals. Brown tied Willie Anderson but lost the play-off with 84 to 82. He made fair sums of money in the United States, partly by playing the stock market, but lost it all in the 1929 Wall Street crash and returned to die in his native Musselburgh.

WILLIE PARK JNR

1887 1889

Born Musselburgh, Midlothian (1864 to 1925). The career of Willie Park Jnr demonstrates changes in the role and status of the professional golfer. The son of a famous father, he was soon involved in club and ball making and won his first tournament at the age of 17. He was 'given' his first Open victory when his closest rival, Willie Campbell, took 9 on the 34th after encountering Prestwick's Cardinal bunker. Park was back at his Musselburgh workbench the next morning. His second Open win also contained a streak of fortune. Andrew Kirkaldy contrived to miss a one-inch putt which allowed Park to catch him and in the play-off Park won convincingly.

The status of Open champion offered business openings. Park threw himself into clubmaking and had shops in London and New York. He was an innovative designer and his bulger driver and wry-necked putter were particularly popular. (Park was renowned for his putting and coined the slogan 'the man who can putt is a match for anyone'.) He also took early opportunities to involve himself in golf architecture. As a result of these activities Park's golfing skills declined but he took part in some famous matches. With the advent of mass manufacture of clubs, he devoted his latter years to course design and construction, working in Britain, Europe and intensively in North America. He is regarded as the first great golf-course architect, with Sunningdale Old being his masterpiece.

JACK BURNS

1888

Born St Andrews, Fife (1859 to 1927). The diminutive Ben Sayers of North Berwick – an excellent player – was one of the most persistent Open competitors but he never quite managed to win the Open. Competing from 1880 to 1923, he came closest at St Andrews in 1888 when he tied with Jack Burns and Davie Anderson with a 36-hole total of 172. While all three prepared themselves for a play-off the following day, there came the sort of scorecard incident that nowadays would cause a furore. Contemporary reports note that it was discovered 'by accident' that Burns's total for his first round in the morning had been put at 87 when it actually amounted to 86. He was therefore declared champion, making him the first player to win when based outside Scotland – he was greenkeeper and professional at Warwick GC and unknown as a player outside St Andrews.

His prize was £8 and a medal. As Burns was so little known, what press there were paid him no attention. His victory was said to have resulted from 'driving long and sure, handling his iron well, and putting deadly'.

Burns's star faded rapidly. The following year he was 25 strokes behind the leader; after a gap, he finished 49 strokes behind in 1894. A plasterer by trade, he gave up professional golf for a steadier job, as a platelayer on the railways. When asked about his golf form in later years he used to reply: 'Never better! I haven't been off the line for years.'

JOHN BALL

1890

Born Hoylake, Cheshire (1861 to 1940). John Ball was the first Englishman and the first of only three amateurs to win the Open, sharing with Bobby Jones the distinction of winning the Open and Amateur Championships in the same year. He first entered the Open in 1878 when, aged 16, he was fifth, a remarkable feat by so young a competitor. Surprisingly, he entered only once more (in 1885, when he did not return his cards) before the 1890 Open. Ball's play at Prestwick was extremely steady, his driving long and straight and his accurate shots to the greens taking the strain off his putting. He had two rounds of 82, four nines in 41 each and no really poor holes. With four holes to play, he knew he had to finish in 20 strokes to win and found the task easy, winning by three. An 11 at the Road hole the following year put him out of contention at St Andrews but he came close again in 1892 at Muirfield. Leading after three rounds, he then had to give way to the brilliance of Harold Hilton, a fellow member of Royal Liverpool whose first headquarters had been in Hoylake's Royal Hotel, owned by Ball's father.

The Open was far less important to Ball than the Amateur Championship in which he competed from its founding in 1885 until 1921, apart from a three-year break while serving in the Boer War. He won a record eight titles between 1888 and 1912, was runner-up twice, and in the all-time rankings of amateur golf only Bobby Jones can be considered his superior.

HUGH KIRKALDY

1891

Born St Andrews, Fife (1868 to 1897). Hugh Kirkaldy's older brother Andrew is a legendary figure in golf – but he never managed to win the Open. This Hugh did at St Andrews the last time the event was played over 36 holes, beating his brother and Willie Fernie by two strokes on a stormy day. Such was his talent that three years earlier he had played the Old Course in 74 (33 out) to knock three strokes off Young Tom Morris's record – and then lowered it again with a 73 the following year. He had a reputation as an aggressive bold player, with a 'beautiful slashing swing', and was said to have become steadier only the year before his victory.

Kirkaldy had a steady record in the Open and was runner-up in 1892 and joint fourth with Andrew in 1893. He took advantage of the opportunities opening up in England and served as professional/greenkeeper at Oxford, Coventry and Silloth, at the last of which, in 1896, he beat J.H. Taylor in his prime in a two-day match. Not long afterwards he caught influenza and this seems to have weakened him for attack by tuberculosis from which he died in St Andrews after a long illness. He was only 29.

In January every year, the Oxford and Cambridge Golfing Society play their annual competition for the President's Putter. The club in question is the wooden-headed putter with which Hugh Kircaldy won the Open and it can be seen in the clubhouse at Rye.

HAROLD HILTON

1892 1897

Born West Kirby, Cheshire (1869 to 1942). It is strange that two men from the same club, Royal Liverpool at Hoylake, should have equally strong claims to be ranked the greatest British amateur. Ball had eight British Amateurs and one Open; Hilton two Opens and four Amateurs. Although he was an all-round player, he was outstanding with his woods, which he could draw and fade as he chose.

Hilton's victory in 1892 came at the Honourable Company's new course, Muirfield, when the format was extended from 36 to 72 holes. He won in brilliant style. After 36 holes he was seven behind the leader but his last two rounds of 72, 74 were exceptionally low for the 1890s and he stormed through the field to win by three strokes. At Hoylake his last-round 75 earned him his second title by one stroke from James Braid who came close to holing a putt on the final hole to tie. Other fine performances came in 1898, when he was third, and in 1911, when he had achieved a winning position but then faltered, finishing a stroke off the Vardon/Massy play-off.

Hilton made many appearances in the Amateur Championship but had to endure defeat in three finals before his first win in 1900 – which he then defended successfully the following year. Perhaps his greatest season was 1911. As well as the near miss in the Open, he won the Amateur and also became the first and still the only British player to win the US Amateur.

WILLIE AUCHTERLONIE

1893

Born St Andrews, Fife (1872 to 1963). One of the youngest to win the Open, Willie Auchterlonie – alas for Scotland – is the last Scottish-born player resident in Scotland to have won the championship. After J.H. Taylor's dazzling first round of 75, Auchterlonie went into the lead after two rounds (78, 81) and his 81, 82 was good enough to give him a two-stroke margin over amateur Johnny Laidlay. It says something about his temperament that he was able to score so well after recording 5, 8, 6 and 6 on Prestwick's par-4 opening hole.

Having served his clubmaking apprenticeship, Auchterlonie won the Open with clubs he made himself (only seven and it is claimed he used only five!) and started his own business, which became D. & W. Auchterlonie. He featured amongst the leaders in the Open only once again, being fifth in 1900. He was far more devoted to clubmaking and remarked: 'It's an awful empty life hitting golf balls every day; you are not giving much service' – not a thought that would be expressed by many modern professionals.

In 1935 he succeeded Andrew Kirkaldy as honorary professional to the R&A and in 1950, with James Braid and J.H. Taylor, he was the first to be made an honorary member of the club. Willie's son Laurie, who also became an excellent clubmaker and was considered an authority on the history of the craft, was made honorary professional on his father's death.

J.H.TAYLOR

1894 1895 1900 1909 1913

Born Northam, Devon (1871 to 1963). A member, with Braid and Vardon, of what came to be known as the Great Triumvirate, John Henry Taylor (but always known as 'J.H.') was almost as evolutionary a player as Vardon. He was, by comparison, no stylist, standing to the ball rather flat-footed and cutting off his follow-through. However, his ability with the mashie, the equivalent of a 5-iron, made watchers realise that they should be trying to stop close to the flag rather than be content to aim at the green. The amount of backspin he could work on the ball was remarkable for his times.

Taylor was the first English professional to win the Open, his victory at Sandwich (the first Open venue outside Scotland) ushering in a new era. Winner again in 1895, he seemed set to dominate the game but Vardon then emerged to displace him in the late 1890s. Taylor first lost to him in a big match and then lost the 1896 Open in a play-off. Taylor went on to win five Opens (in 12 top-three finishes) and many tournaments and matches but it was Vardon again who denied him a sixth Open in 1914 after he had entered the final round with a two-stroke lead.

A self-educated man, Taylor became a fine writer and was a prime mover in the development of the PGA. After serving as professional at Burnham, Winchester, Wimbledon and – for over forty years – Royal Mid-Surrey, he retired to a hill overlooking Westward Ho! where he had caddied at 11.

HARRY VARDON

1896 1898 1899 1903 1911 1914

Born Grouville, Jersey, Channel Islands (1870 to 1937). The most celebrated member of the Great Triumvirate, Harry Vardon changed people's conception of how well the game could be played. His playing method – which included an overlapping grip, slightly open stance, bent left arm and upright but effortless rhythm – was unorthodox for the times. The long, flat slashing 'St Andrews swing', with a loose grip at the top, was the norm. Vardon's methods were copied. It is said that he never missed a fairway with his driver and that his faded fairway woods and long irons always covered the flag. What was truly revolutionary about the methods of Vardon, as well as Taylor and Braid, was that they held onto the club firmly at the top of the backswing.

Vardon's peak years were 1896 to 1900 when few could cope with his mastery of the gutty in either matchplay or strokeplay events. People flocked to see him in tournaments and exhibition matches up and down the country and he made an equal impression in the United States when he undertook a strenuous tour there in 1900. He returned as US Open champion.

Shortly after winning his fourth Open Vardon developed tuberculosis and his results declined. Eventually, however, he recovered his form and won two more Opens including a record sixth in 1914. Only a strong wind and fatigue prevented him from winning the 1920 US Open.

JAMES BRAID

1901 1905 1906 1908 1910

THE OPEN CHAMPIONSHIP AT MUIRFIELD, JUNE 1906. JAMES BRAID (CHAMPION)

Born Earlsferry, Fife (1870 to 1950). The figures above show just how dominant Braid was in his peak years from 1901 to 1912. By 1901 Harry Vardon and J.H. Taylor had each won the Open three times yet it was Braid who became the first of them to win the championship five times. During that golden spell he was also runner-up twice and never worse than sixth. He won the French Open in 1910 and, an excellent matchplayer, he took the PGA Matchplay Championship in 1903, 1905, 1907 and 1911. Even when he was 57 he managed to reach the final, losing to Archie Compston.

Braid was a long hitter, one who suddenly found much increased distance overnight. He was described as hitting 'with divine fury' and if he was sometimes erratic he was also blessed with tremendous powers of recovery, particularly from bunkers. Early in his career, his putting was suspect when he used a cleek. It was transformed when he took to a Mills aluminium-headed club which was successfully marketed in later years as the Braid-Mills.

He became professional at Romford in 1896 and in 1904 moved to newly opened Walton Heath where he remained for the rest of his life. He was also in great demand as a golf architect and designed or reshaped hundreds of courses, mainly in England and Scotland, including the King's and Queen's courses at Gleneagles.

SANDY HERD

1902

Born St Andrews, Fife (1868 to 1944). Apprenticed first to a baker and then to a plasterer, Sandy Herd became a professional golfer at the age of 23. He won three tournaments that same year and tied second in the Open. From then on he was often threatening to win, especially at St Andrews in 1895 and Muirfield in 1896, when he started off with the amazingly low score of 72 (the equivalent of, say, a 62 today).

When victory eventually came, it was particularly historic. Herd was the first champion to use the 'modern' wound ball, a Haskell. Playing a practice round with John Ball, he was given one to try on the 15th tee and immediately hit the longest drive of his life. Legend has it that Herd played with one Haskell throughout and that rubber strands were dangling before the championship ended. (He was, in fact, able to buy four from the Hoylake professional.) After a sound opening of 77, 76 he took a three-stroke lead on the final morning with a brilliant 73 in strong winds when his closest rivals, Braid and Vardon, could manage only 80s. Herd was far less convincing in the afternoon but an 81 still saw him home by a stroke.

At the age of 52, Herd managed a second place in 1920, having held the joint lead after three rounds, but his most remarkable feat of 'old age' was to win the PGA Matchplay Championship at the age of 58. He made his last Open appearance in 1939, a span of 54 years.

JACK WHITE

1904

Born Dirleton, East Lothian (1873 to 1949). From 1894 to 1914 the Great Triumvirate of Vardon, Braid and Taylor dominated the Open Championship, winning 16 of the 21 events in that period. One of the few to break their stranglehold was Jack White, the nephew of Ben Sayers. White scored progressively lower rounds – 80, 75, 72, 69 – and his aggregate of 296 at Sandwich was the first time the 300 barrier was broken in the event. Braid, with 69 and 71 on the final day, made a desperate attempt to catch him as did Taylor whose last round of 68 was the lowest of the championship. This was phenomenal scoring with Braid's third round being the first ever to break 70 in the championship. Both finished a stroke behind.

White never made a strong showing in the championship in the years after. However, his victory was the climax of a good spell in the event. He was runner-up behind Vardon in 1899, fourth in 1900, sixth in 1901 and third behind the Vardon brothers in 1903.

White was a native of North Berwick but spent most of his career in the south where he worked as professional to various clubs before joining in 1902 the newly opened Sunningdale where he was to remain for 25 years. Sunningdale marked his Open win by giving him a pay rise, a rent-free cottage and £75. Later he became a well known clubmaker and eventually retired to Scotland.

ARNAUD MASSY

1907

Born Biarritz, France (1877 to 1958). A French Basque, Massy was early a sardine fisherman but began to caddie, mostly for English visitors. Playing golf himself quickly followed. He modelled his game on one of the visitors, Horace Hutchinson. He used a two-handed grip and an open stance. A powerful man, he was a long hitter and highly thought of as a cleek player. He went to North Berwick to complete his golfing education and the local professional, Ben Sayers, promptly declared he would soon win the Open. He made an immediate impact in the Open by finishing 10th on his first appearance in 1902. He was fifth in 1905 and sixth in 1906.

The weather was foul at Hoylake in 1907 but Massy had the game to combat the hurricane winds and sheeting rain. He led, or tied for the lead, throughout and had the extra satisfaction of beating J.H. Taylor, the best bad-weather player of them all, by two strokes. In so doing he became the first overseas player to win the Open. During the championship his wife gave birth to a daughter, whom they christened Hoylake.

Massy came close to winning another Open in 1911 when he made up four strokes on Vardon to tie at Sandwich. In the play-off, however, he conceded on the 35th. He bounced back quickly, crossing the Channel to win one of his four French Opens by seven strokes with all the top players in the field. He remains the greatest French golfer ever.

TED RAY

1912

Born Grouville, Jersey, Channel Islands (1877 to 1943). Ted Ray has some claim to be considered the first power hitter ('sluggers', Walter Hagen later called them). The strengths of his game were vast driving, powerful recoveries and, as so often with this kind of player, a delicate touch in the short game.

It was because of the great contrast in their styles that Harry Vardon twice toured the United States with him. They moved across the country taking on the best local professionals and amateurs and were seldom beaten. Vardon reeled off the pars and Ray the birdies and bogeys. In 1913, the pair tied for the US Open with Francis Ouimet and great was the shock when they lost the play-off to the 20-year-old amateur. On a repeat visit in 1920, Vardon should have won it but it was Ray who actually did so, the last such success by a British player until Tony Jacklin's win in 1970.

Ray, several years younger than the Great Triumvirate, began to emerge in 1903, reaching the final of the prestigious PGA Matchplay Championship. Soon he was also proving a consistent performer in the Open and at Muirfield in 1912 he took the first-round lead and was never threatened thereafter, winning by four strokes. After several years at Ganton, he became professional at Oxhey in 1912 and remained there for the rest of his life.

[34]

GEORGE DUNCAN

1920

Born Oldmeldrum, Aberdeenshire (1883 to 1964). Despite the higher scoring seventy years ago, caused by rougher course conditions and less effective equipment, you still didn't expect to win an Open if you started off with a couple of 80s – especially if you were 13 strokes behind the leader (Abe Mitchell). Yet Duncan made up the whole of that deficit with a 71 while Mitchell staggered to an 84. Duncan had bought a new driver before the third round and it really suited him. It continued to do so in his cast-iron final round of 72.

In 1922, Duncan produced another sensational performance in the Open. Walter Hagen had played an excellent final round of 72 and it seemed to be all over when news came from out on the course that Duncan, despite the bad weather, was playing the round of a lifetime, except that he wasn't converting all his good birdie chances. Eventually, he came to the last needing a par 4 to tie but managed only a 5 on the very difficult 18th at Royal St George's. His 69 was the first round below 70 since 1904.

Duncan emerged as a force to be reckoned with a few years before the First World War. He was famous for the speed of his play but with a swing modelled on Vardon's he lasted a long time and was still able to trounce Hagen, his opposing captain, by 10 and 8 in the 1929 Ryder Cup singles.

He and Abe Mitchell were the leading British players in the 1920s.

JOCK HUTCHISON

1921

Born St Andrews, Fife (1884 to 1977). One of many St Andrews men who emigrated to make a career in the United States, Hutchison had the great satisfaction of winning on his home course to become, ironically, America's first Open champion. His victory, during the first round of which he holed in one at the 8th and nearly repeated the feat at the 9th, was slightly controversial. The bite on his approach shots was extreme and it was noticed that the roughly punched faces of his irons might be against the spirit of the game, if not the rules at that time. Hutchison did not win outright, despite an exceptional final round of 70. The English amateur Roger Wethered tied by playing the golf of his life on the final day for scores of 72 and 71 – but he was no match for Hutchison in the 36-hole play-off.

Hutchison was at his peak either side of the First World War and came close to winning the US Open several times. Between 1911 and 1923 he was in the top five on five occasions, including runner-up in 1916 and joint runner-up in 1920. In 1916 he lost by one hole to Jim Barnes in the final of the very first USPGA Championship but made amends in 1920.

Late in life, Hutchison again became a familiar face on the golfing scene. The Masters begins with a ceremonial nine holes played by two great figures from the past and for many years the pair were Hutchison and Freddie McLeod.

WALTER HAGEN

1922 1924 1928 1929

Born Rochester, New York, USA (1892 to 1969). Walter Hagen was one of golf's great characters, a flamboyant showman whose remarks such as 'Never hurry, never worry and always remember to smell the flowers along the way' and 'Miss a putt for two thousand dollars? Not likely!' are part of golfing lore. He was also a very great golfer even if technically far from perfect, with a swing, they used to say, that started with a sway and ended with a lunge. This may account for why he played more very bad shots in a round than a Vardon or Hogan would have expected to play in a year. However, he would dismiss such errors immediately and tackle the problems ahead.

Hagen was supreme as a putter and his short game was excellent. Few could match his nerve over the closing holes of a championship. He won the 1914 and 1919 US Opens, then stormed Britain in the 1920s with four wins, a second and a third out of eight starts in the Open.

Hagen was probably at his best as a matchplayer. Between 1921 and 1927 he entered the USPGA Championship six times. He won in 1921, was runner-up in 1923, then took four in a row. In a showdown with Bobby Jones in 1926, Hagen won by 11 and 10. He had equal disasters, losing by 18 and 17 to Archie Compston (whom he beat shortly afterwards in the 1928 Open) and by 10 and 8 to George Duncan in the 1929 Ryder Cup singles. Former caddie Hagen didn't mind. The defeat would make good headlines.

ARTHUR HAVERS

1923

Born Norwich, Norfolk (1898 to 1981). When Havers won his champion-ship at Troon it was not the occasion for national rejoicing. Americans had yet to achieve total dominance but this was the last British victory until Henry Cotton's first success 11 years later. Havers's win was a narrow one, by a single stroke over the holder, Walter Hagen. The championship presentation was very sparsely attended. Hagen was annoyed that Troon (like most other clubs at this time) did not allow professionals into the clubhouse. When he was asked in for the presentation, Hagen politely de-clined and instead invited the crowd to accompany him to the local pub for a drink.

Havers was certainly not a great champion, perhaps because of a defec-tive grip. Four knuckles showed on the left hand and his right apparently did little more than hold the club. Combined with a hand position well ahead of the clubhead, this sometimes led to a severe fit of shanking.

As champion, Havers went over to the United States and managed to beat Bobby Jones and Gene Sarazen in challenge matches, both major achievements. He won few tournaments and was seldom in contention during the Open but he did have the satisfaction of posting the lowest round (68) of the championship in 1932. He represented Great Britain against the United States five times.

JIM BARNES

1925

Born Lelant, Cornwall (1887 to 1966). 'Long' Jim Barnes (he was 6ft 4in) emigrated to the United States in his late teens. A frequent competitor in the Open during the 1920s, he had many good finishes. His 1925 victory, however, is remembered more for the man who lost, Macdonald Smith, a Carnoustie-born man who had also gone to America. Smith began his final round with a five-stroke lead but it seemed that the whole of Scotland had come to see him win. The stewards lost control of the 15,000 crowd and Smith lost control of his golf game. He was not helped by the fact that he thought the unruly behaviour of the crowd was intended to distract him.

Barnes, playing three hours ahead of Smith, had set the target just as Smith started out. It stood up, Barnes winning by a stroke from Ted Ray and Archie Compston. Smith, after an 82 when he never saw the result of a single long shot, came in fourth, three strokes behind. The founder of the Open, Prestwick has never hosted another. As is the case with Hoylake, the final holes are too close together to accommodate large crowds.

Barnes might have been somewhat fortunate to win this title but no such luck was needed in his US Open victory in 1921. He led after each round and won by nine strokes, still the record. He also won the first two USPGA Championships, was twice losing finalist to Hagen, and had nearly 20 victories in America.

BOBBY JONES

1926 1927 1930

Born Atlanta, Georgia, USA (1902 to 1971). Arguably the most dominant player of all time, Jones won about half of all the tournaments he entered from his competitive debut at the age of 14 until his retirement aged 28 in 1930. His record in the British Open is perfect after a disastrous start when he tore up his card during the third round at St Andrews in 1921. He made three more entries and won the lot.

Jones won the US Amateur five times, the US Open four times and the British Amateur once in three entries. The reasons for his success are many. He was immensely competitive and at his best in a tight finish, sometimes losing concentration if he found himself with a big lead. Technically, his swing was much admired because of its lazy rhythm and his putting from long range had exquisite touch and good judgement and he missed little from short range. The only apparent weakness in his golfing armoury was that he was not an outstanding pitcher of the ball but he overcame all that in his Grand Slam year of 1930 when he won the Amateur and Open titles on both sides of the Atlantic. With no worlds left to conquer, he then retired to a life in the law and business.

The best golf writer to have also been a great golfer, Jones was largely responsible for founding one of the world's greatest courses, Augusta National, and the Masters.

TOMMY ARMOUR

1931

Born Edinburgh (1895 to 1968). A Walker Cup team member in 1922, Tommy Armour – 'The Silver Scot' – stayed on in the United States after the match and turned professional a couple of years later. He won his first major title, the US Open, in 1927. A birdie on Oakmont's final hole, a very tough par 4, took him into a play-off with Harry Cooper which he won by three strokes.

By this time Armour was legendary as a superb iron player. He himself thought his driving better. It was very accurate so he left himself with less to do for the shot to the green.

In his Open victory over the difficult Carnoustie, Armour seemed to have lost his chance with a third-round 77 which put him five strokes behind José Jurado and Macdonald Smith, but he played brilliantly in the final round until missing a short putt on the 17th. Faced with another on the last, Armour held his putter as tightly as he could and remarked afterwards: 'From the instant the club left the ball on the backswing I was blind and unconscious.' It went in and secured him his third major. His second had come at the expense of Gene Sarazen in a thrilling final in the 1930 USPGA Championship.

As his career went into natural decline, Armour switched to high-priced golf teaching and also wrote two hugely successful instruction books.

GENE SARAZEN

1932

Born Harrison, New York, USA (1902). Gene Sarazen – who changed his name from Saraceni because he thought it made him sound like a violin player – is the longest surviving Open champion, followed by Sam Snead with whom he played a few ceremonial holes at the Masters up to 1991.

Sarazen arrived young, winning the 1922 US Open at 20 years 4 months and taking the USPGA Championship the same year, a success which he repeated in 1923 when he beat Walter Hagen in the final. Further victories eluded him until, having 'invented' the sand iron, his greatest year arrived in 1932. He went into the Open at Prince's, Sandwich, the favourite and led throughout, winning by five strokes. (His aggregate of 283 stood as the record until 1950.) A fortnight later he won the US Open. He had a poor start of 74, 76 but suddenly began to play brilliantly midway through the third round. He had a 70 followed by a 66 and won by three strokes. Bobby Jones described it as 'the finest competitive exhibition on record'.

In the 1935 Masters Sarazen played the most famous golf shot of all. On the 15th, he needed to birdie three of the last four holes to catch Craig Wood, leader in the clubhouse. For his second shot over water to this par 5 he rode into a 4-wood, holed out for a double eagle and won the play-off the next day. He was back in the headlines in 1973 when he holed in one at Troon's Postage Stamp during the Open.

DENSMORE SHUTE

1933

Born Cleveland, Ohio, USA (1904 to 1974). How fortune can change in golf. Shute's experiences in the 1933 Ryder Cup matches at Southport and Ainsdale could have scarred him for life. On the last hole of his singles, the decisive one, with Syd Easterbrook, he took three to reach the green on a relatively easy hole and then, still with a putt to win the Ryder Cup, rattled it past the hole and missed the return.

Apparently unscarred, he then went off to St Andrews and won the Open. The Old Course was bone-hard that year and therefore playing short (Craig Wood drove into a bunker 430 yards out on one hole). But it wasn't easy because of fast glassy greens and the luck of the bounce on so many shots. Shute had four rounds of 73 and tied Craig Wood before winning the play-off with some ease.

Shute also tied the 1939 US Open with Byron Nelson and Wood but lost the play-off. He won the USPGA in 1936 and 1937 and in that last year took part in a famous 72-holes challenge match at Walton Heath against Henry Cotton, which he lost. He played on three Ryder Cup teams and was particularly successful in 1931, winning his foursomes match by 10 and 9 and his singles 8 and 6. Although Shute was never a tournament regular, opting for the relative security of club jobs, he won 10 US Tour events in his short career.

HENRY COTTON

1934 1937 1948

Born Holmes Chapel, Cheshire (1907 to 1987). Cotton was recognised as the outstanding British player from about 1929 but he fumbled his chances in the Open for several years. It suddenly came right when he began at Royal St George's in 1934 with rounds of 67 and 65, a remarkable 36-hole total that stood as the record until the deeds of Faldo and Norman at St Andrews in 1990. After a solid 72, he went into the final afternoon with a nine-stroke lead and played very badly for 12 holes. With the title fast slipping away, Cotton then found his game again and won by five shots.

With little American interest in the Open at the time, Cotton's win was perhaps tarnished. However, his triumph at Carnoustie in 1937 was achieved against the combined strength of America's Ryder Cup team.

Cotton came from a middle-class background and had been to public school – then unheard of amongst professional golfers. As champion, he dressed the part and lived in some style. After the Second World War he was relatively hard up and his Muirfield victory helped to restore his fortunes. Winning by five strokes, he posted a new course record of 66.

He ended his days at Penina, the course he had designed on what had been paddy fields in Portugal's Algarve. A great champion of the cause of the professional golfer, he died in the knowledge of his forthcoming knighthood, awarded absurdly late.

ALF PERRY

1935

Born Coulsden, Surrey (1904 to 1974). A surprise winner in 1935, Perry is one of the few golfers not of major championship calibre to win the Open in modern times. One writer remarked unkindly that 'he came from nowhere and then went back there'. So saying, you cannot fault the manner of Perry's victory at Muirfield. After a start of 69, 75 he shot into the lead with a 67 and then played a very steady 72 to win by four strokes from Alf Padgham, whose turn lay just ahead. Perry's aggregate equalled the record and the way in which he finished was remembered for many a year. With no fuss at all he banged woods into the last two greens when others might have played safer with an iron towards the front of each of the greens.

Perry's technique would be much frowned upon today. He had his right hand too much under the shaft and played the ball too far from his body. However, Bernard Darwin remarked that 'he wallops the ball with a gorgeous and whole-hearted confidence'. He also had a very good short game. Perhaps his best year was 1938 when he won three tournaments, in one of which he managed to play Wentworth with all four rounds under 70. Although not generally a strong performer in the Open, he did have one other chance of winning, in 1939, when he finished joint third after a last round of 76.

He played on three Ryder Cup teams in the 1930s with little success.

ALF PADGHAM

1936

Born Caterham, Surrey (1906 to 1966). From early in his career, Padgham was thought to possess the purest of golf swings, as good as Vardon or Snead. He took the club back lazily and then poured the clubhead through the ball with no apparent effort. This meant an outstanding long game and his chipping was also excellent. Putting, however, was a great weakness – until Padgham decided to use his chipping technique, the ball well away from his body. Soon he was sweeping them all into the hole and his Open victory came during the best two years or so of his career, during which he had a record four consecutive victories.

His first two rounds of 73 and 72 at Hoylake left him one off the lead. On the final day he found his clubs were locked in the pro's shop – a brick through the window and an apology later solved that one. He went round in 71 which he knew put him in hot contention. However, with two rounds being played, the leaders not going out last, and the system of recording scores in terms of par well into the future, the situation was seldom entirely clear. When Padgham went out on his final round, well before lunchtime, his three-round total put him a stroke behind what Henry Cotton and Jimmy Adams would post at the same stage. His 37 out wasn't good but a fine burst just afterwards earned him another 71. Adams came closest to matching the target, missing a putt to tie on the last.

REG WHITCOMBE

1938

Born Burnham, Somerset (1898 to 1958). The Whitcombe brothers set a record in 1935 when three of them – Ernest, Charles and Reg – played in the 1935 Ryder Cup matches. Charles was considered the best striker of his times but never quite managed to take the Open.

Reg didn't reach his peak until approaching the age of 40. He then enjoyed a very good few years in the Open. In 1937, at Carnoustie, he led Henry Cotton by three strokes with a round to go. In foul weather he then finished with a 76 to Cotton's magnificent 71. Perhaps Reg was a little discouraged when his driver flew out of his wet hands on one tee shot, but he managed second despite a strong American contingent.

If anything, the weather was worse at Royal St George's the following year. The first two days were fine and after two rounds Reg was two strokes behind leaders J.J. Busson and Bill Cox, but on the final day there was probably the strongest wind ever to blow in an Open Championship. It destroyed the main exhibition tent and made golf almost impossible. The joint leaders failed to break 80 in their four rounds and there were tales of players being unable to reach par 4s with three good driver shots. One player complained that he cracked a 1-iron over the Suez Canal on the 14th only to see the ball blown back into it. In these circumstances, Reg's 75 (the best morning round) and 78 brought him a deserved victory by two shots.

DICK BURTON

1939

Dick Burton and Sam Snead during the 1949 Ryder Cup at Ganton

Born Darwen, Lancashire (1907 to 1974). It is often said that the Americans stopped entering the Open after the early 1930s. In fact there were usually three or four top players from across the Atlantic but in 1939 there was only that frequent contender, Johnny Bulla. In a high-scoring championship, Burton's start of 70, 72 gave him the lead but he lost ground with a 77 and began the final round four strokes behind Johnny Fallon, with many others in contention. He then produced a fine 71, two strokes better than anyone else, to win by two strokes from Bulla.

Burton's play on the final hole at St Andrews was much admired. In order to avoid slicing into the town, most competitors tend to aim left from the tee even though the approach shot is easier from the right. Burton scorned safety and drove down the line of the rails, lofted a 9-iron and holed the putt. His final action was casually to toss his putter to his caddie once he thought his putt was right for pace and line.

As Open champion, Burton was guaranteed at least modest pickings from product endorsement and exhibition matches but the Second World War soon put paid to that and he had to be content with the longest reign of any Open winner, seven years. He played on three Ryder Cup teams either side of the war and in 1949 set a (then) aggregate record for a British tournament of 266 with rounds of 68, 66, 64 and 68.

SAM SNEAD

1946

*Sam Snead (driving) and Gene Sarazen, the longerst surviving
Open champions, during the 1986 Masters*

Born Hot Springs, Virginia, USA (1912). Snead came close to winning the US Open at his first attempt yet one of the most illustrious of careers was to remain blemished by his failure to capture that title. There were many near misses, the most famous being in 1939 when he needed a par 5 on the last to win and took an 8. In 1947, he lost a play-off to Lew Worsham, a missed short putt on the last hole being to blame.

Ironically, Sam Snead placed little value on his British Open title. He had to be persuaded to come and entered mainly to help Wilson's promote sales of his signature clubs in Britain. After his victory at St Andrews he described the event as 'just another tournament', did not defend the following year or indeed enter again until his peak years were long past.

Snead's swing on full shots was the epitome of lazy rhythm combined with great power and he was also one of the best wedge players ever. Later in his career he suffered a putting twitch which, with moderate success, he combatted by putting between his legs, croquet-style. When this was banned by the R&A and USGA, he switched to a similar technique. He still faced the hole with the ball outside his right foot.

Snead won three Masters titles and three USPGAs, a record 81 US Tour events and more than 130 victories in all. He was Ryder Cup captain in 1951 and 1959 and non-playing captain in the tied match of 1969.

FRED DALY

1947

Born Portrush, Ireland (1911 to 1991). The only Irishman to have won the Open, Daly is also the last winner to have had a really high score in one of his rounds. After opening with 73 and 70 (when he seemed to chip dead or hole a good putt on nearly every hole), Daly held a four-stroke lead. Then came a 78 which reduced him to a share of the lead with three other players as he set off on his final round, ahead of most of the contenders. His golf to the turn was not inspired. He then put in a good burst which included an amazing 3 at Hoylake's short 13th. He topped his tee shot into a pit in front of his nose, managed to get his next to the edge of the green and then his hickory-shafted putter with rusty blade got the ball into the hole from some 20 yards. His putter again helped him when he holed from a dozen yards to birdie the last, one of the longer putts to win an Open.

He had set a good target but the ending of the championship was sensational. American amateur Frank Stranahan needed a 2 to tie on the par-4 18th and failed to hole his 9-iron by mere inches.

Daly lost some of his best years to the Second World War but was brilliant after it for several years. He recorded other fine performances in the Open but was at his best in matchplay, winning the PGA Matchplay Championship three times and proving a most effective Ryder Cup player – he won his singles in 1953 by 9 and 7.

BOBBY LOCKE

1949 1950 1952 1957

Born Germiston, South Africa (1917 to 1987). Of all the great champions, Locke was the most unlikely-looking of them all. Many professional golfers are overweight but they seem also to look brawny with it. In Locke's case he merely looked flabby, an impression aided by his very leisurely gait up the fairways of the world.

His swing was one of the most unorthodox in modern times to bring success. He crossed the line to extremes at the top, aimed many yards right of target and then hooked every shot back into play and at the flag. In his youth he had faded the ball but he then adopted the hook in order to obtain maximum length with a minimum of force. Some said he even hooked his putts – an impossibility. That he was one of the best putters of all time is, however, undisputed.

Locke first made his name in 1947 when he won six events on the US Tour, the most sensational season ever by an overseas player. The following season he set a record which still stands when he won an event by 16 strokes. Animosity was shown towards him so he played most of his competitive golf thereafter in Europe and South Africa.

His three Opens in four years made him a commanding figure until he was displaced by Peter Thomson. Locke brought the Australian's run to an end with his victory in 1957.

MAX FAULKNER

1951

Born Bexhill, Sussex (1916). Faulkner was an unhappy man when play began in 1951 at Royal Portrush (the only time the championship has not been played in Scotland or England). His short game was working well enough but he was plagued by a slice that was so bad that kindly fellow professionals wouldn't play him for money in practice rounds. Always an experimenter, Faulkner set off with a very light putter which had a pencil-slim shaft and grip. As putt after putt dropped, his long game began to improve. By the end of the second day his 71, 70 had put him two strokes in the lead and he was declaring that he would never miss a short putt again – and greatly tempting fate by signing autographs 'Open Champion 1951'.

The gods were kind and a round of 70 on the final morning stretched his lead to six strokes. In the afternoon he played with great authority most of the way and a few dropped shots later on were not enough to prevent his victory, the last by a British player until 1969.

Faulkner was as famous for his flamboyance and eccentricity as for his splendid play. He was the first British tournament player to wear highly colourful clothes, which always earned him as much press coverage as his play. He never used a matched set of clubs and was said to own 300 putters, the most unusual of which was made from a snooker cue with a driftwood head.

BEN HOGAN

1953

Born Dublin, Texas, USA (1912). Hogan is one of the few to win the Open at his first (and only) attempt. Had he not already won the Masters and the US Open in the same year it is unlikely that he would have made the journey, but come he did. Always the perfectionist, he took the job very seriously, allowing himself plenty of time to get to know Carnoustie and to adjust his technique to the different demands of links golf. After two days, he faced the 36 holes of the final day two behind the leaders and a 70 in the morning took him to the top of the leader board with de Vicenzo. His last round had the stamp of inevitability about it. He played some outstanding golf for a 68, winning the championship by four strokes. Such was the quality of his play that Bernard Darwin reckoned he could have shot a 64 if that was what was needed to win.

This is the only time that three of the professional titles have fallen to one man in the same year and confirmed his status as one of golf's all-time greats. In fact, Hogan played only five times in 1953 and won on each occasion. He restricted his play in order to focus attention on the majors as he knew he had limited resources as a result of severe injuries in a car smash early in 1949. Before that, he was a prolific tournament winner, with 13 events to his name in 1946, 10 in 1948 and 63 Tour wins in all. Included amongst these were four US Opens, two Masters and two USPGAs.

PETER THOMSON

1954 1955 1956 1958 1965

Born Melbourne, Australia (1929). The first Australian to win the Open, Thomson is also the player who has come closest to equalling both Vardon's six victories and Young Tom Morris's four in a row.

In the 1950s, his consistency still amazes. From 1952 to 1958 his finishes were 2nd, 2nd, 1st, 1st, 1st, 2nd, 1st. At the end of this sequence he was still under 30 with all the records at his mercy. He then began to show human weakness, sometimes starting with a poor first round and at other times finishing unconvincingly when in hot contention. People began to point out that Thomson's achievements had come in a period when there was never a strong American presence and that he had also failed to make serious impact on the US Tour.

Over the years, Thomson had the answer. In 1965, he took his fifth title with all the great performers in the field, including Nicklaus, Palmer and the holder, Lema. Success in the United States came very much later, on the Senior Tour which has grown so rapidly since 1980. Retired from competitive golf for some time, Thomson didn't make serious efforts in the Seniors until his mid-50s. He began to establish himself again in 1984 and broke all records the following year.

Amongst the most intelligent of champions, Thomson always had wider interests than simply playing tournament golf.

GARY PLAYER

1959 1968 1974

Born Johannesburg, South Africa (1935). With over 120 tournament victories worldwide, Player has a phenomenal record, beaten only by Sam Snead and Roberto de Vicenzo (some of whose wins were not against top fields). His victories include nine majors, placing him fourth behind Nicklaus (20), Jones (13) and Hagen (11); five World Matchplays; seven Australian Opens; and an incredible 13 South African Opens. All this from a man who was advised to give up professional golf when he first appeared in Europe as it was thought that he had a poor swing and grip and no feel for the game. But Player persevered. He became the best bunker artist of all time while the rest of his game had no real weaknesses. A short man, he worked extremely hard to build his body in order to achieve greater distance off the tee and, as he said, 'The more I practise, the luckier I get.'

Player's first major was the 1959 Open at Muirfield which he thought he had thrown away with a double bogey on the last. At Carnoustie in 1968 he fought off Nicklaus's challenge to come through by two strokes. However, his finest performance in the Open was at Lytham where he played superb golf in difficult conditions to become the first to win with the big ball. He reserved his best victory to the end when he birdied seven of the last 10 holes to take the 1978 Masters (his third) with a final round of 64. Then aged 42, he is now – not surprisingly – a successful senior golfer.

KEL NAGLE

1960

Born North Sydney, Australia (1920). Nagle was a late developer who did not establish himself until he changed his game. Previously a long but wild hitter, he became much shorter but very steady and was an outstanding putter. Even so, he was an outsider for the Centenary Open at St Andrews. His fellow Australian, Peter Thomson, had great faith in his abilities and both encouraged him and bet on him.

Nagle's win was achieved under extreme pressure. With opening rounds of 69 and 67 he was still two adrift of Roberto de Vicenzo but had reversed that position by the final round. The main threat to his lead was expected to come from Arnold Palmer, making his debut in the Open and four behind but fresh from his last-round charge of 65 to take the US Open. Having also won the Masters, he was in with a chance of the modern version of the Grand Slam. Palmer attacked from the start but Nagle produced birdies of his own. The climax came on the 71st hole. Ahead, Palmer birdied the last while Nagle faced a par putt of a couple of yards or so. He got it and then calmly parred the last to win by one stroke.

Two years later Nagle was the only man to threaten Palmer's almost total control of the championship and in 1965 he tied for the US Open, losing the play-off to Gary Player. Altogether he won more than 30 events around the world and went on to more success in seniors golf.

ARNOLD PALMER

Born Latrobe, Pennsylvania, USA (1929). Professional golfers and some of the governing bodies of golf owe Palmer a great debt. His charismatic appeal, with his power and boldness, started the revival of the British Open, raising it to its pre-eminence today. In the United States, he vastly increased public interest in the US Tour and – later – the Senior Tour.

Palmer's impact on the Open was immediate. In 1960 he came over as recently crowned US Open champion and made a great run at the Centenary Open at St Andrews, finishing second behind Kel Nagle. The following year he played some superhuman golf in foul weather and won at Birkdale. For an encore, he then played the greatest major championship of his career at Troon. Only Nagle could keep in touch and he lost by six strokes with the third-place men 13 in his wake.

While he retained his powers for several more years, Palmer was never again in serious contention for the Open. His championship career came to almost as abrupt an end in the United States. He won four Masters titles between 1958 and 1964, yet no more came his way. One of his strengths had been bold putting; when he lost his confidence on the short returns his greatest days were over and he had to concede superiority to Nicklaus.

Palmer won 60 events on the US Tour and another 19 overseas. More recently he has had 10 Senior Tour successes.

BOB CHARLES

1963

Born Carterton, New Zealand (1936). The only lefthander – and New Zealander – to win a major championship, Charles took the lead at Lytham after breaking the course record with a 66 in the third round. The final round was between Charles, Phil Rodgers and Jack Nicklaus, who faltered at the end, leaving the other two to contest a play-off. Charles was a convincing winner (69, 71 to 72, 76), enquiring afterwards if 18 holes weren't really enough – and so it came to pass for many years. In 1968 Charles was joint-second in the Open; the following year he posted another 66 at Lytham but had to settle for second place behind Tony Jacklin.

The crucial factor in Charles's success was his putting. He was evolutionary in this department, the first performer reckoned outstanding to take the wrists out of his stroke. The world was soon copying him though not with such success – he once played 11 tournament rounds before a three-putt green. Such was his reputation as a putter that many people failed to notice his other great strength, steadiness through the green.

Charles won the 1954 New Zealand Open as an amateur but caution prevented his turning professional for six years. He won 24 events worldwide and is now amassing another, greater, fortune on the US Senior Tour. His deportment on the course is impeccable: no dramatics, just a touch at the peak of his eye shade to acknowledge applause.

TONY LEMA

1964

Born Oakland, California (1934 to 1966). The life expectancy of a golfer must be well above the average but Lema's career was cut short in 1966 by a crash in a small plane. It was only a couple of years after he had established himself as one of the top three or four in the game.

The achievement largely responsible for this was his victory at St Andrews and the manner of it. Lema arrived the day before play started with time only for a hurried practice round, perhaps not even a whole one. 'Never mind', he decided, he would hit the ball from the tee in the directions indicated by his caddie, Tip Anderson, who would also have to club him for the shots to the greens. After an opening 73, Lema took charge with a 68 while his greatest threat, Jack Nicklaus, began 76, 74. He stumbled for the first few holes of the third round while Nicklaus played brilliantly, but then came good and was round in 68. On the final afternoon, he played serenely for a 70 and won by five strokes. The following year he led after the first and second rounds and was in contention to the end – but this was a Thomson year.

Lema was an elegant swinger, a master of the pitch shot and knew how to finish the hole with his putter. Accused early in his career of being more interested in partying than his stroke average, he later earned the nickname 'Champagne' because he presented a case to the press after his wins.

JACK NICKLAUS

1966 1970 1978

Born Columbus, Ohio, USA (1940). The greatest player of all time? Nicklaus's record in major championships (20 wins and so often in close contention) is such that the majority of modern commentators rank him as their number one. He cannot play Young Tom Morris, Vardon, Jones and Hogan but he has proved himself the best in an age when there are more very good players than ever before.

For 17 years he was never out of the top four in the USA, where only Sam Snead won more than his 70 tournaments to which should be added another 18 wins worldwide. In the major championships his victories spanned 27 years from the 1959 US Amateur to the 1986 Masters. Brilliant play over the last 10 holes – six birdies and an eagle – brought him his sixth Masters title at the age of 46.

A very long hitter in his younger days, Nicklaus's greatest playing strengths were his long-iron play and putting. He was not so good from sand and he felt that he lacked variety of shots and touch around the green. His mental approach was outstanding. He studied a course intently, deciding where to try to place all his shots, when to attack and when to defend. His greatest strength of all was his mental toughness which meant that in the cauldron of the last few holes with a championship in the balance Nicklaus very seldom threw one away.

ROBERTO DE VICENZO

1967

Born Buenos Aires, Argentina (1923). 'How about that amigo? I come back to see my friends and I win ze bloody championship!' Roberto de Vicenzo was a majestic swinger of the golf club and perhaps the best striker in the world for many years. His Achilles heel was his putting. When things were going well he still lacked confidence on the greens and it sometimes evaporated entirely. Even so, his superb talents have won him 39 national championships and a total of tournaments variously estimated but certainly more than 150.

In the Open, he had finished second or third six times since his debut in 1948 but he just couldn't win, not even after a start of 67, 67 at St Andrews in 1960. So when he came to Hoylake in 1967, talk was all of the holder, Nicklaus, Player and whether Thomson could equal Vardon's total of six victories. But de Vicenzo found a putting stroke which worked that week. He took a two-stroke lead with a third round of 67, Player collapsed and Nicklaus's final 69 wasn't good enough. Roberto finished as he had played throughout, his long game superb and his putting not letting him down. It was one of the Open's most popular triumphs.

Disaster followed nine months later. Having tied the Masters with a final round of 65, it was found that his marker had put down '4' for the 17th instead of a 3. He had signed his card; the 4 had to stand.

TONY JACKLIN

1969

Born Scunthorpe, Lincolnshire (1944). The first European in modern times to show that Americans are not invincible, Jacklin was one of very few to make full campaigns on the US Tour. By winning the Jacksonville Open in 1968, he became the first British golfer to win in the United States since Ted Ray in 1920. His British Open win was the first by a Briton since Max Faulkner in 1951. Jacklin had been playing fairly poorly in America when he arrived at Lytham for the championship but a start of 68, 70 gave him confidence. He was three strokes behind Bob Charles but after a 70 in the third round he went two ahead and maintained that position to the end. The vast drive he hit dead straight up the last fairway will be long remembered, yet it was probably his secure short putting and superb bunker play that contributed most.

His victory in the US Open was a greater achievement. It came in 1970 and included the rare feat of leading from start to finish. His seven-stroke margin made him seem a world-beater. His bitter failure to win at Muirfield in 1972, when Lee Trevino chipped in three times in 21 holes, proved to be the start of a long slow decline and Jacklin never contended again in a championship. He later enjoyed even greater renown as the captain of four Ryder Cup teams and was in charge for the first defeat of the United States since 1957 and the first ever success on American soil.

LEE TREVINO

1971 1972

Born Dallas, Texas, USA (1939). When Trevino came from total obscurity to win the 1968 US Open, some thought this could well be the only tournament of any kind he would win. The reason was his outrageous swing. Keeping a strong left hand grip he plays with a wide open stance, driving through his legs and pulling the clubface through with his arms to counteract the fact that his clubface is shut at the top.

In 1970 Trevino was leading US money-winner and in 1971 he took his second US Open after a play-off with Jack Nicklaus. He followed up with the Canadian Open title and then fought out the British Open with Lu Liang-Huan and Tony Jacklin. Trevino's putting was superb but, with the title in his pocket, he took 7 on the 71st but still got home by a stroke.

His win at Muirfield in 1972 was more memorable. In his third-round 66 he finished with five birdies in a row, full of long putts, holed chips and even a thinned bunker shot which clattered into the flag and then dropped into the hole. With Trevino playing the par-5 17th of the final round badly, the odds were on Jacklin – until Trevino chipped in once again.

Trevino has also won the USPGA Championship in 1974 and 1984 amongst his 27 US Tour wins and has several international titles. In his first season on the US Senior Tour he won seven events and $1,190,518 – more than the leading money-winner on the full Tour.

[63]

TOM WEISKOPF

1973

Born Massillon, Ohio, USA (1942). Once thought the best swinger and striker in the game, Weiskopf had an ultimately disappointing career for his apparent destiny to be a great player was never quite fulfilled. His victory at Troon came in his best season. Going into the third round he had a three-stroke lead following rounds of 68 and 67. He was paired with Johnny Miller who overtook him for a while but he closed the day one stroke ahead and was never seriously threatened thereafter. It was his fifth win in eight events.

That year Weiskopf seems to have been highly motivated – something he always found difficult – and kept a hot temper under control. He once remarked that 'desire to win is the necessary thing', an attribute perhaps lacking in his own attitude to the game. He viewed the US Tour as a means of paying for his greater passion, hunting, and once turned down a Ryder Cup place for this reason.

The winner of 15 US Tour events and another half-dozen overseas, Weiskopf also came close to US Open titles and was runner-up in the Masters in 1969, 1972, 1974 and 1975. The last of these was a classic, with Weiskopf and Miller both missing birdie chances to tie Jack Nicklaus on the final green. Five years later, Weiskopf had the misfortune to record a 13 at Augusta's very difficult par-3 12th.

TOM WATSON

1975 1977 1980 1982 1983

Born Kansas City, Missouri, USA (1949). When Watson achieved his fifth Open title at Birkdale in 1983 he was still only 33 years old and well within reach of Vardon's record six titles. The following year, he again came close when Ballesteros's brilliance and a Watson error on the 71st hole saw the championship slip away. He has not been the same player since and has won but a single tournament out of a career total of some 40 events.

Watson had long been ranked the best there was on and around the greens but he lost his putting touch, increasing the pressure on the rest of his game. So saying, Watson at his peak always had that rare ability to raise his game for the big occasion and he still sometimes manages to get close in the majors, as in the 1987 US Open, the 1989 Open and the 1991 Masters.

Watson won at Carnoustie in 1975 on his first appearance in the Open. In 1977 Turnberry witnessed one of the greatest championships of all time as Watson (65, 65) and Jack Nicklaus (65, 66) engaged in a head-to-head duel over the last 36 holes. His performance at Muirfield in 1980 was equally impressive and included a 64. At Troon in 1982 he was handed the title as others wilted but the following year he needed to par Birkdale's long closing hole. A superb 2-iron to the heart of the green clinched matters.

Watson also has the 1982 US Open on his record, famous for his chip-in from the fringe on the 71st, and the 1977 and 1981 Masters.

[65]

JOHNNY MILLER

1976

Born San Francisco, California, USA (1947). 'Happiness is when you know that even your worst shots are going to be quite good.' This was the Miller of 1974 and 1975 when he played golf to a standard which has never been clearly bettered. During that period he won 12 of his 23 US Tour events. People said that he was better than Jack Nicklaus and for a time he seemed certain to establish himself as the world's number one.

A leading player by the early 1970s, Miller grabbed the headlines in the 1973 US Open. After a steady first two rounds, he put himself out of contention with a 76 – or so it seemed. He was six strokes behind. But not when he opened up with four birdies in the final round and continued to give himself chance after chance. He accumulated five more, shot a 63 and was champion. His play in the 1975 Masters was almost as dramatic. After two rounds, he was 10 strokes off the lead. His finish of 65, 66 was the lowest in the tournament's history and brought him to within one stroke of Nicklaus. When he won the Open the following year at Birkdale he was just beginning to pass his peak but he won in style. His final round of 66 gave him victory by six strokes from Nicklaus and the suddenly emerging Seve Ballesteros, whose recovery play during the week had been extraordinary.

Miller is virtually retired from competitive golf now and much involved in golf course architecture.

SEVE BALLESTEROS

1979 1984 1988

Born Pedrena, Spain (1957). All three of Severiano Ballesteros's victories have been high drama, reflecting the excitement the man creates on a golf course – even if going round in 75. After becoming the youngest Open champion this century, some Americans labelled him 'the car park champion' because his final-round tee shot at Lytham's 16th finished amongst BBC vehicles. It is true that he hit few fairways and some very wild shots but his powers of recovery were phenomenal and became his trademark.

His victory at St Andrews was different. He hardly dropped a shot to par and this time avoided all the bunkers. With the contest in the balance between the Spaniard and Tom Watson, Ballesteros's finish was decisive. He managed a par at the impossible Road hole and then birdied the last and Latin emotions flowed. Back at Lytham in 1988, he raced into the lead with a 67 in difficult weather but come the final round it was a contest between new leader Nick Price, Ballesteros, Faldo and Lyle. The last two eventually faded and Ballesteros seized the title with a course record of 65.

By winning the 1980 Masters, Ballesteros heralded a new era that has seen a steady shift of power from America to Europe. He added another Masters title in 1983 and can number 63 wins worldwide, many of them on the hugely successful European Tour. Whether smiling or scowling, he remains – like Arnold Palmer with whom he is so often compared – the star attraction.

BILL ROGERS

1981

Born Waco, Texas, USA (1951). Although only 40 in 1991, Rogers was by this time appearing very rarely on the US Tour, where he had been a nonentity since 1983. In his strange career, he had only two outstanding seasons, 1979 and 1981. In the latter year he was the world's most successful golfer, winning three times in the United States with other victories in Japan, Australia and, of course, at Royal St George's. In one phase, he had five wins in six appearances.

Rogers had finished joint second in the US Open and his friend Ben Crenshaw urged him to enter the Open but he came close to disqualification when he misread his teeing-off time. After a 66 he took the lead at the end of the second day and a 67 gave him a five-stroke margin going into the final round. He stumbled with three bogeys in his first eight holes but then hit back with a run of birdies. His only problem came when, nearing the last green, he was mistaken for a spectator and stopped by a policeman.

What went wrong afterwards? Some blamed his management for giving him far too much to do in 1981; others pointed to the fact that, although he was an outstanding putter, the rest of his game was marred by a suspect grip. For whatever reason he went into a sudden decline and after the last of five US Tour wins he quickly lost all confidence. A golfer may reach the top but success can come and go overnight.

SANDY LYLE

1985

Born Shrewsbury, Shropshire (1958). For many years Lyle and Nick Faldo contended for public attention as best British golfer (not forgetting Ian Woosnam). Lyle reached the major targets first. In 1985 he became the first British player to win the Open since Tony Jacklin in 1969. His win at Royal St George's came when none of the contenders were able to make a strong move, all dropping shots instead. Lyle's break came with birdies on the 14th and 15th which gave him a share of the lead. For a time it looked as if he had thrown it all away when he took three to get down from just off the final green but others faltered as well.

In 1988 Lyle achieved another landmark by becoming the first Briton to win the Masters. The bunker shot that he played from 140 yards out to set up his birdie on the 72nd green provided one of golf's great moments. By the end of that year, he had easily the best record of any British player in the United States with five wins (as compared to Ballesteros's six). He had also shown his relaxed attitude to both money and fame by making little effort to be crowned leading money-winner on the US Tour, preferring instead to play most of his golf in Europe.

Lyle's loss of form came early in 1989. Many blamed his swing, which is most unusual, with the club first swung very low, then lifted to the top followed by a downswing that owes almost everything to hands and arms.

GREG NORMAN

1986

Born Mt Isa, Queensland, Australia (1960). If Sam Snead's career blemish was his failure to win the US Open, Norman's, as a prolific winner of tournaments, is his lack of victories in the majors. Some have been cruelly snatched from his grasp by fluke shots, such as Bob Tway's short bunker shot on the 72nd hole of the 1986 USPGA Championship and Larry Mize's chip from nearly 50 yards on the second play-off hole in the 1987 Masters. Yet Norman himself has quite often faltered in the majors. Tway may have been lucky but Norman went into the final round with a four-stroke lead and had scored three bogeys and two double bogeys before Tway did for him. Other examples are the 1986 Masters, in which he hit his iron to the last green wildly right into the crowd, thus failing to tie Nicklaus; and the 1989 Masters in which he also bogeyed the last to miss the Hoch/Faldo play-off.

In 1986 Norman led all the majors after three rounds and his British Open title contained some magnificent play. In very bad weather, he managed a first-round 74 and then took the lead with a 63 to equal the championship record. In the fourth round his partner Tsuneyuki Nakajima made a mess of the 1st and 3rd holes and Norman shot into a lead of five and cruised home in some comfort. That year his winnings on the world golf circuit were over $1 million. He was US leading money-winner for a second time in 1990, by the end of which he had totalled 58 wins worldwide.

NICK FALDO

1987 1990

Born Welwyn Garden City, Hertfordshire (1957). With four major championships to his credit, Faldo can well claim to be the greatest British player since the far-off days of the Great Triumvirate. Those who would point to the name of Cotton should note that he seldom cared to compete in the United States and his achievements there were negligible.

There are strong contrasts in the ways that Faldo has won his majors. At Muirfield in 1987 he ground out a round with every hole in par and was 'given' that Open when Paul Azinger collapsed on the last two holes. His consecutive victories in the Masters also had an element of chance. In 1989, during the sudden-death play-off, Scott Hoch missed a tiny putt for victory and the following year Ray Floyd pulled an iron shot into water at the same stage. Faldo's finest hour to date is undoubtedly his Open victory at St Andrews. After a brilliant start of 67, 65 he was tied for the lead with Greg Norman and then destroyed him with a 67 to the Australian's 76. On the final day Faldo was faced with the prospect of ludicrous failure if he had thrown away his five-stroke lead but his play was unwavering.

Much has been made of Faldo's swing changes and it was certainly courageous to risk losing his game altogether. We shall never know if he would have won those majors with his old swing. However, his short-game skills have been equally valuable in taking him to the very top.

MARK CALCAVECCHIA

1989

Born Laurel, Nebraska, USA (1960). Once a player has got himself into contention in a tournament, the actual winning often depends on somebody else's blunder or a fluke shot. In 1988, for example, Calcavecchia was readying himself for a play-off for the Masters with Sandy Lyle after Lyle bunkered his tee shot at the final hole, needing a par 4 to tie. Yet Lyle whisked that 7-iron from the sand to a puttable distance and got a 3 to win outright. A year later, and the British Open, and Calcavecchia benefited from a blunder by Greg Norman who failed to realise he might reach a fairway bunker with his driver on the last of the four play-off holes.

First qualifying to play the US Tour in 1981, Calcavecchia had to wait until 1986 for his first win but since then he has always been in the top ten, amassing over $3 million on the Tour with successes elsewhere, the highpoint of his career coming at Troon. Always in touch with the leaders, yet not considered likely to win, a long putt on the 11th and a lob from a bank into the hole on the next improved his prospects and he won the play-off with a superb second shot to the last.

In times when so many US Tour players are said to lack star appeal and are even unrecognisable due to their sponsors' eye-shades, Calcavecchia stands out with his distinctive swing. An extremely long hitter, he lashes at the ball and seems to move much of the golf course along with it.

IAN BAKER-FINCH

1991

Born Nambour, Queensland, Australia (1960). Ian Baker-Finch hit the headlines back in 1984 when opening rounds at St Andrews of 68 and 66 took him to a three-stroke lead in the Open. He had the best putting stroke on view and after a 71 went into the final day tied with Tom Watson. There followed a nightmare round of 79 which included a pitch to the first green that spun back into the Swilcan Burn. He made no real impact on the Open again until 1990 when a third-round 64 put him in a tie for second place at St Andrews. Paired with Nick Faldo, who held on to his five-stroke lead, he took 73 and finished sixth. He said afterwards, 'All I did was eat dust. Faldo taught me I needed to be tougher, to focus on what I am out there to do, rather than on what's going on around me.'

His 64 in the third round at Birkdale in 1991 meant that, once again, he was last out on the final day but it was Ballesteros, a couple of strokes behind, who was the favourite, with the derisory odds of 33-1 being offered on the leader. However, the charge came not from Seve but from Baker-Finch who birdied five of the first seven holes to be out in 29, a rare feat. His 66 displayed the mettle of a champion and he finished two strokes ahead of his fellow Australian, Mike Harwood.

Baker-Finch has won in Australasia, Japan and the United States but only once before in Europe. He now plays the US Tour full time.

OPEN CHAMPIONS

† 12-hole course   ‡ two rounds of 9-hole course   * amateur

YEAR	VENUE	WINNER					SCORE	WM
1860	† Prestwick	Willie Park Snr	55	59	60		174	2
1861	† Prestwick	Tom Morris Snr	54	56	53		163	4
1862	† Prestwick	Tom Morris Snr	52	55	56		163	13
1863	† Prestwick	Willie Park Snr	56	54	58		168	2
1864	† Prestwick	Tom Morris Snr	54	58	55		167	2
1865	† Prestwick	Andrew Strath	55	54	53		162	2
1866	† Prestwick	Willie Park Snr	54	56	59		169	2
1867	† Prestwick	Tom Morris Snr	58	54	58		170	2
1868	† Prestwick	Tom Morris Jnr	51	54	49		154	5
1869	† Prestwick	Tom Morris Jnr	50	55	52		157	11
1870	† Prestwick	Tom Morris Jnr	47	51	51		149	12
1871	No competition							
1872	† Prestwick	Tom Morris Jnr	57	56	53		166	3
1873	St Andrews	Tom Kidd	91	88			179	1
1874	‡ Musselburgh	Mungo Park	75	84			159	2
1875	† Prestwick	Willie Park Snr	56	59	51		166	2
1876	St Andrews	Bob Martin	86	90			176	–

Martin tied with Davie Strath who refused to play off

1877	‡ Musselburgh	Jamie Anderson	82	78			160	2
1878	† Prestwick	Jamie Anderson	53	53	51		157	2
1879	St Andrews	Jamie Anderson	84	85			169	3
1880	‡ Musselburgh	Bob Ferguson	81	81			162	5
1881	† Prestwick	Bob Ferguson	53	60	57		170	3
1882	St Andrews	Bob Ferguson	83	88			171	3
1883	‡ Musselburgh	Willie Fernie	75	84			159	–

Fernie won play-off with Bob Ferguson 81, 77 to 82, 77

1884	Prestwick	Jack Simpson	78	82			160	4
1885	St Andrews	Bob Martin	84	87			171	1
1886	‡ Musselburgh	David Brown	79	78			157	2
1887	Prestwick	Willie Park Jnr	82	79			161	1
1888	St Andrews	Jack Burns	86	85			171	1
1889	‡ Musselburgh	Willie Park Jnr	78	77			155	–

Park won play-off with Andrew Kirkaldy 82, 76 to 85, 78

1890	Prestwick	*John Ball	82	82			164	3
1891	St Andrews	Hugh Kirkaldy	83	83			166	2
1892	Muirfield	*Harold Hilton	78	81	72	74	305	3
1893	Prestwick	Willie Auchterlonie	78	81	81	82	322	2

[74]

YEAR	VENUE	WINNER					SCORE	WM
1894	Sandwich	J.H. Taylor	84	80	81	81	326	5
1895	St Andrews	J.H. Taylor	86	78	80	78	322	4
1896	Muirfield	Harry Vardon	83	78	78	77	316	–
		Vardon won play-off with J.H. Taylor 78, 79 to 80, 81						
1897	Hoylake	*Harold Hilton	80	75	84	75	314	1
1898	Prestwick	Harry Vardon	79	75	77	76	307	1
1899	Sandwich	Harry Vardon	76	76	81	77	310	5
1900	St Andrews	J.H. Taylor	79	77	78	75	309	8
1901	Muirfield	James Braid	79	76	74	80	309	3
1902	Hoylake	Sandy Herd	77	76	73	81	307	1
1903	Prestwick	Harry Vardon	73	77	72	78	300	6
1904	Sandwich	Jack White	80	75	72	69	296	1
1905	St Andrews	James Braid	81	78	78	81	318	5
1906	Muirfield	James Braid	77	76	74	73	300	4
1907	Hoylake	Arnaud Massy (Fr)	76	81	78	77	312	2
1908	Prestwick	James Braid	70	72	77	72	291	8
1909	Deal	J.H. Taylor	74	73	74	74	295	6
1910	St Andrews	James Braid	76	73	74	76	299	4
1911	Sandwich	Harry Vardon	74	74	75	80	303	–
		Vardon won play-off with Arnaud Massy who conceded at 35th hole						
1912	Muirfield	Ted Ray	71	73	76	75	295	4
1913	Hoylake	J.H. Taylor	73	75	77	79	304	8
1914	Prestwick	Harry Vardon	73	77	78	78	306	3
1915-9	No competition							
1920	Deal	George Duncan	80	80	71	72	303	2
1921	St Andrews	Jock Hutchison (USA)	72	75	79	70	296	–
		Hutchison won play-off with Roger Wethered 74, 76 to 77, 82						
1922	Sandwich	Walter Hagen (USA)	76	73	79	72	300	1
1923	Troon	Arthur Havers	73	73	73	76	295	1
1924	Hoylake	Walter Hagen (USA)	77	73	74	77	301	1
1925	Prestwick	Jim Barnes (USA)	70	77	79	74	300	1
1926	Lytham	*Bobby Jones (USA)	72	72	73	74	291	2
1927	St Andrews	*Bobby Jones (USA)	68	72	73	72	285	6
1928	Sandwich	Walter Hagen (USA)	75	73	72	72	292	2
1929	Muirfield	Walter Hagen (USA)	75	67	75	75	292	6
1930	Hoylake	*Bobby Jones (USA)	70	72	74	75	291	2
1931	Carnoustie	Tommy Armour (USA)	73	75	77	71	296	1
1932	Prince's	Gene Sarazen (USA)	70	69	70	74	283	5
1933	St Andrews	Densmore Shute (USA)	73	73	73	73	292	–
		Shute won play-off with Craig Wood (USA) 75, 74 to 78, 76						
1934	Sandwich	Henry Cotton	67	65	72	79	283	5
1935	Muirfield	Alf Perry	69	75	67	72	283	4
1936	Hoylake	Alf Padgham	73	72	71	71	287	1

YEAR	VENUE	WINNER					SCORE	WM
1937	Carnoustie	Henry Cotton	74	72	73	71	290	2
1938	Sandwich	Reg Whitcombe	71	71	75	78	295	2
1939	St Andrews	Dick Burton	70	72	77	71	290	2
1940-5	No competition							
1946	St Andrews	Sam Snead (USA)	71	70	74	75	290	4
1947	Hoylake	Fred Daly	73	70	78	72	293	1
1948	Muirfield	Henry Cotton	71	66	75	72	284	5
1949	Sandwich	Bobby Locke (SA)	69	76	68	70	283	–
	Locke won play-off with Harry Bradshaw 67, 68 to 74, 73							
1950	Troon	Bobby Locke (SA)	69	72	70	68	279	2
1951	Portrush	Max Faulkner	71	70	70	74	285	2
1952	Lytham	Bobby Locke (SA)	69	71	74	73	287	1
1953	Carnoustie	Ben Hogan (USA)	73	71	70	68	282	4
1954	Birkdale	Peter Thomson (Aus)	72	71	69	71	283	1
1955	St Andrews	Peter Thomson (Aus)	71	68	70	72	281	2
1956	Hoylake	Peter Thomson (Aus)	70	70	72	74	286	3
1957	St Andrews	Bobby Locke (SA)	69	72	68	70	279	3
1958	Lytham	Peter Thomson (Aus)	66	72	67	73	278	–
	Thomson won play-off with Dave Thomas 68, 71 to 69, 74							
1959	Muirfield	Gary Player (SA)	75	71	70	68	284	2
1960	St Andrews	Kel Nagle (Aus)	69	67	71	71	278	1
1961	Birkdale	Arnold Palmer (USA)	70	73	69	72	284	1
1962	Troon	Arnold Palmer (USA)	71	69	67	69	276	6
1963	Lytham	Bob Charles (NZ)	68	72	66	71	277	–
	Charles won play-off with Phil Rodgers (USA) 69, 71 to 72, 76							
1964	St Andrews	Tony Lema (USA)	73	68	68	70	279	5
1965	Birkdale	Peter Thomson (Aus)	74	68	72	71	285	2
1966	Muirfield	Jack Nicklaus (USA)	70	67	75	70	282	1
1967	Hoylake	Roberto de Vicenzo (Arg)	70	71	67	70	278	2
1968	Carnoustie	Gary Player (SA)	74	71	71	73	289	2
1969	Lytham	Tony Jacklin	68	70	70	72	280	2
1970	St Andrews	Jack Nicklaus (USA)	68	69	73	73	283	–
	Nicklaus won play-off with Doug Sanders (USA) 72 to 73							
1971	Birkdale	Lee Trevino (USA)	69	70	69	70	278	1
1972	Muirfield	Lee Trevino (USA)	71	70	66	71	278	1
1973	Troon	Tom Weiskopf (USA)	68	67	71	70	276	3
1974	Lytham	Gary Player (SA)	69	68	75	70	282	3
1975	Carnoustie	Tom Watson (USA)	71	67	69	72	279	–
	Watson won play-off with Jack Newton (Aus) 71 to 72							
1976	Birkdale	Johnny Miller (USA)	72	68	73	66	279	6
1977	Turnberry	Tom Watson (USA)	68	70	65	65	268	1
1978	St Andrews	Jack Nicklaus (USA)	71	72	69	69	281	2
1979	Lytham	Seve Ballesteros (Sp)	73	65	75	70	283	3

YEAR	VENUE	WINNER					SCORE	WM
1980	Muirfield	Tom Watson (USA)	68	70	64	69	271	4
1981	Sandwich	Bill Rogers (USA)	72	66	67	71	276	4
1982	Troon	Tom Watson (USA)	69	71	74	70	284	1
1983	Birkdale	Tom Watson (USA)	67	68	70	70	275	1
1984	St Andrews	Seve Ballesteros (Sp)	69	68	70	69	276	2
1985	Sandwich	Sandy Lyle	68	71	73	70	282	1
1986	Turnberry	Greg Norman (Aus)	74	63	74	69	280	5
1987	Muirfield	Nick Faldo	68	69	71	71	279	1
1988	Lytham	Seve Ballesteros (Sp)	67	71	70	65	273	2
1989	Troon	Mark Calcavecchia (USA)	71	68	68	68	275	–
		Calcavecchia won 4-hole play-off with Greg Norman						
1990	St Andrews	Nick Faldo	67	65	67	71	270	5
1991	Birkdale	Ian Baker-Finch (Aus)	71	71	64	66	272	2

INDEX OF NAMES

Main entries in italic

PICTURE ACKNOWLEDGEMENTS

The editor and publishers would like to thank the following individuals and organisations for allowing their illustrations to be included in this book: All-Sport pages 65, 67, 73 (David Cannon), 72 (Simon Bruty); Associated Sports Photography/E.D. Lacey pages 55, 62; Sarah Baddiel Collection pages 28, 30; Cowie Collection and St Andrews University pages 11, 13, 16, 19, 31, 46, 53, 59; Michael Hobbs Collection pages 10, 14-5, 17-8, 20-7, 29, 32-3, 35-8, 40-1, 43-4, 47-8, 50, 56, 70; Provincial Press Agency page 61; Royal & Ancient Golf Club of St Andrews pages 42, 45, 54; Phil Sheldon pages 49, 60, 63, 66, 68, 69, 71 (Karina Hoskyns), 72; Sotheby's page 12; Sport and General Press Agency page 58; Bob Thomas pages 57, 64; United States Golf Association page 39. The paintings reproduced in the book are the work of the following artists: Willie Park Snr (page 10) by John A. T. Bonnar; Harold Hilton (page 56) by Richard Jack (Royal Liverpool club); Walter Hagen (page 37) by Frank C. Bensing (USGA); Henry Cotton (page 44) by John A. A. Berrie (R&A).